AWESOME INVENTIONS
You Use EVERY DAY

STINKY SANITATION INVENTIONS

KATIE MARSICO

LERNER PUBLICATIONS COMPANY
MINNEAPOLIS

Lerner Publications Company
A division of Lerner Publishing Group, Inc.
241 First Avenue North
Minneapolis, MN 55401 U.S.A.

Website address: www.lernerbooks.com

Library of Congress Cataloging-in-Publication Data

Marsico, Katie, 1980—
Stinky sanitation inventions /
by Katie Marsico.
p.   cm. — (Awesome inventions you use every day)
Includes index.
ISBN 978-1-4677-1090-9 (lib. bdg. : alk. paper)
ISBN 978-1-4677-1686-4 (eBook)
1. Sanitation—Technological innovations—Juvenile
literature. 2. Hygiene—Technological innovations—
Juvenile literature. 3. Public health—Technological
innovations—Juvenile literature. 4. Environmental
health—Technological innovations—Juvenile
literature. 5. Inventions—Juvenile literature. I. Title.
RA567.M38   2014
363.72—dc23   2012048758

Manufactured in the United States of America
1 – BP – 7/15/13

CONTENTS

KEEP IT CLEAN

Sometimes life stinks. Sometimes you have to get your hands dirty. And sometimes you have to take out the trash.

Those might sound like a bunch of lines from a detective movie, but the world can be a smelly place. People come in contact with harmful germs every day. And for most of human history, garbage trucks weren't around to drive off with our messes. Believe it or not, our ancient relatives didn't even have toilet paper.

For hundreds and hundreds of years, scientists and engineers have come up with ways to keep people healthy and smell-free. So have some clever inventors working at home. Get ready for the stories behind twelve odor-stopping, germ-blocking inventions. You'll find out why the world would *really* stink without them.

FLUSHABLE TOILETS

Heads up! If you had lived in medieval England, you wouldn't have wanted to be standing under the castle garderobe while the local lord or lady was doing his or her business. This closetlike room stuck out from castle walls. A garderobe featured a tiny opening through which waste dropped. The royal business usually landed in a disgusting moat below.

In the late 1500s, going to the bathroom became slightly less gross—and more sanitary. At that time, the writer Sir John Harington of England described a version of the toilet in one of his books. He pictured a small tank raised above the ground. Harington's invention had two features of the modern toilet. Water flowed through the tank's piping. A valve got the water moving. Harington didn't just write about his invention, either. He installed his toilets in some fancy houses, including the home of his godmother, Queen Elizabeth I.

A couple hundred years later, other inventors built on Harington's idea. They created the flushable toilet. By the late 1700s, this innovation was all the rage in several parts of the world. These days, even astronauts depend on flush technology. Because of the lack of gravity in outer space, NASA (National Aeronautics and Space Administration) toilets rely on air (rather than water) to flush. Vacuum technology directs the flow of waste. This prevents waste from floating throughout the cabin. The air used to tuck the waste away later moves through the cabin once again—after being very thoroughly cleaned.

Waste has a long way to drop in this model of a medieval garderobe.

UNTIL THE TWENTIETH CENTURY, MOST PEOPLE IN THE UNITED STATES COULDN'T AFFORD ANY KIND OF TOILET—FLUSHABLE OR NOT. An average family was more likely to have an outhouse. An outhouse is a small shanty in the backyard, built over a hole in the ground. If someone heard the call of nature in the middle of the night or during a raging thunderstorm, he or she could stay indoors and use the chamber pot. People kept this bowl-shaped container near the bed, just in case.

PORTABLE TOILETS

When you gotta go, you gotta go! That's what inventors of the portable toilet realized during the 1940s. Shipyard workers of the time faced an urgent problem. Every time a worker needed to take a bathroom break, he had to rush off the ship and back to the docks. This solution wasn't convenient or comfortable. Then a shipbuilder in Long Beach, California, talked to the company that emptied the dock toilets.

A large number of workers soon breathed a sigh of relief. The company set up wooden sheds with tanks inside on board the half-built ships. The rest is porta-potty history. Placing portable toilets at outdoor worksites and events became a popular business. At first, these toilets were made out of wood and metal. Later, designers realized that light materials such as fiberglass and plastic made the potties easier to carry. Modern plastic porta-potties use chemicals to block odors and break down waste.

These chemical toilets go by a wide variety of names, including Porta-John, Tidy John, and Biffs. But no matter what they're called, a wide range of people depend on them—including the president's staff! When Barack

Obama took office in 2009, a record-breaking five thousand porta-potties were rented. The Presidential Inaugural Committee set them up to aid anyone who needed to answer nature's call during the swearing-in ceremony.

TOILET PAPER

The average person goes through almost twenty-one thousand sheets of toilet paper each year. Before this incredible product, people relied on everything from leaves to corncobs while wiping. Paper made solely for use in the bathroom dates back to fourteenth-century China. Chinese emperors commanded that it be produced in sheets that measured a whopping 2 feet (0.6 meters) by 3 feet (0.9 m)!

Toilet paper as we know it got its start in 1857. U.S. inventor Joseph Gayetty began selling "medical" tissue meant to soothe sores and swelling. Gayetty was so proud of the paper that he had his name printed on every sheet. But he didn't have many customers. During the late 1800s, it was considered bad manners to talk about bodily functions. People who wanted to try the new invention were embarrassed to ask for it!

In 1890 brothers Clarence and E. Irvin Scott started making toilet paper on rolls. But they worried that the product would ruin the reputation of their successful paper company. So they decided to sell it in secret, through other, smaller companies. Attitudes finally began to change after 1928. A new company called Charmin started marketing toilet paper as a fashionable luxury item.

Since then people have come to depend on toilet paper—and not just for keeping clean. In the 1960s, colored toilet paper added a decorative touch to bathrooms. These days, though, you won't find toilet paper in any color but white. Pink, blue, and lavender tissues went by the wayside when it turned out that the dyes bothered sensitive skin.

FEW PEOPLE WHO HAVE TOILET PAPER CAN IMAGINE LIFE WITHOUT IT. That's why, in 1973, Americans panicked when TV host Johnny Carson joked that there might be a toilet paper shortage in the United States. Viewers rushed to stock up on T.P. By the next day, supermarkets across the country had indeed run out! Carson soon explained that he'd only been joking—but his joke had created an actual shortage. As soon as shelves were restocked, frantic customers emptied them again. It took three weeks to end the scare.

Horse-drawn carriages carry toilet paper across London in the 1890s.

DRAYTON MILL
Toilet Papers

DRAYTON MILL
Toilet Papers

PAPER WORKS

DRAYTON PAPERS

DISPOSABLE DIAPERS

Ever had to change your baby brother's diaper? Ick! Now pretend you're changing diapers in the 1500s. You might want to plug your nose. Back then, babies only wore diapers made of cloth. And it wasn't unusual for them to go unchanged for days at a time!

Cloth diapers were many people's go-to choice for hundreds of years. The soft fabric probably felt more comfortable than animal skin, moss, leaves, or any of the other materials that had also been used to cover kids' bottoms. Even so, cloth diapers weren't a simple solution. People had to clean and disinfect the cloths to prevent babies from getting sick (and to avoid unpleasant odors).

Luckily, a breakthrough invention took place in the 1940s. Swedish manufacturers began developing the first disposable diaper in 1942. Four years later, Marion Donovan of the United States created an improved model. Her diaper combined the traditional cloth diaper with shower curtain plastic. Donovan's diaper also featured plastic snaps instead of the sharp safety pins that had held cloth diapers in place. By 1948 companies were producing disposables on a large scale.

These days, babies sport disposable diapers that biodegrade (break down naturally) and show off the latest designer trends. Some can even be flushed down the toilet! (Experts estimate that 18 billion diapers end up in U.S. landfills every year. People with an eye toward the future go green by picking the biodegradable variety.)

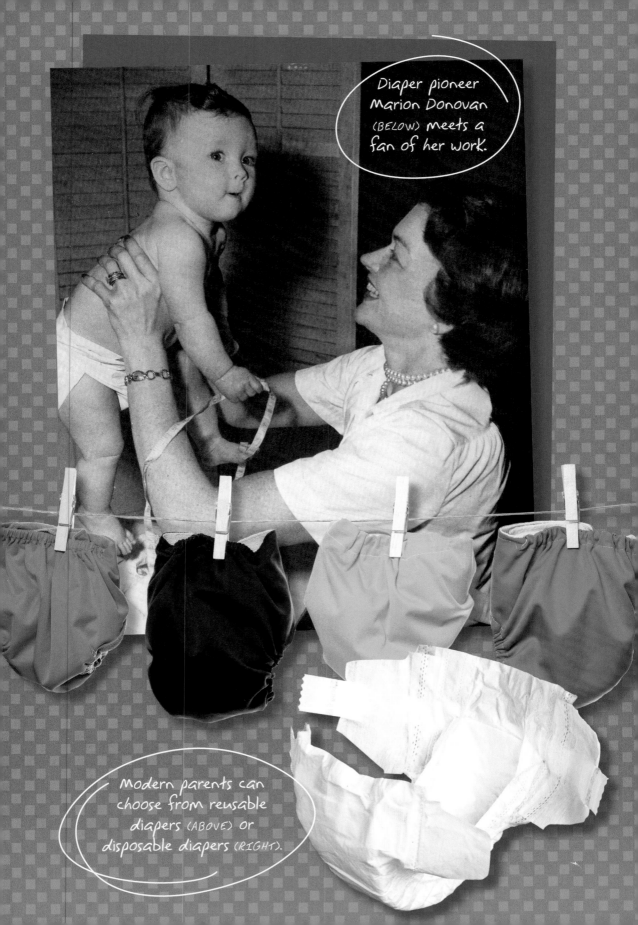

SEWERS

London, England, in the mid-nineteenth century was a dangerous place to be. An infection of the intestines called cholera claimed tens of thousands of lives. The city was thrown into a panic. At first, many medical experts believed the illness was caused by airborne germs. But scientist John Snow determined that the true culprits were bacteria from London's Thames River. A few hundred years ago, London lacked a decent sanitary sewer system. People drank and bathed in sewage-filled water.

Historians suspect that ancient cities used sanitary sewers as early as 8000 B.C.E. Human waste was probably channeled through the sewers to nearby creeks. But by the Middle Ages (ca. 500–1500), most attempts at maintaining such systems had gone down the drain. Sewage typically collected in cesspools or wherever else people could dump it. As countless Londoners realized during the 1800s, the results of these unsanitary methods was disaster.

After a while, engineers figured out how to control the flow of human waste. One solution was a larger version of the sewers that were already in place for storm water. By the early 1900s, several cities had also started to treat sewage before simply flushing it atop local lakes or waterways. Researchers figured out that the use of filters and disinfectants such as chlorine reduced the amount of harmful bacteria found in city plumbing.

Modern sanitary sewers are underground systems of connected pipes. These pipes carry water, human waste, and toilet paper to treatment plants. Ever seen a manhole and wondered where it leads? City workers use these openings to get into the tunnels below.

This modern sewer tunnel in Rhode Island is 300 feet (91 m) underground.

WE CAN CONTROL WHAT GETS FLUSHED DOWN OUR TOILETS AND INTO A SANITARY SEWER SYSTEM. But can we always control what crawls up the plumbing? Sewer rats are a big problem for some communities in the United States. These pesky critters have been known to make their way through the pipes and into the toilet bowl!

London's Thames River was crawling with nasty bacteria in the 1800s.

POOPER-SCOOPERS

C'mon, admit it. You cringe every time your parents remind you that *you* agreed to pooper-scoop the yard when you begged to get a dog. So what is wrong with just letting Fido's business sink back into the soil? Well, experts say that a single gram (0.03 ounces) of doggie doo can hold up to 23 million fecal bacteria. These sickening stowaways can cause major health problems for humans.

Look at the bigger picture for a second. If you collected a few days' worth of puppy poop from about one hundred dogs,

 you'd have a deadly dose of bacteria on your hands. In fact, the Environmental Protection Agency (EPA) estimates that that much bacteria would be enough to ruin the water across a 20-mile (32-kilometer) stretch! So Brooke Miller of California developed an extremely important invention when she designed the pooper-scooper during the 1970s.

Miller's device was basically a metal bin, or scooper, with rakelike hooks. It attached to a wooden stick. This early model also included a rake that pulled waste into the scooper and a hatch that attached to a garbage bag around the base. These days, people can find many versions of the classic pooper-scooper. And dog lovers who don't fancy long walks with a scooper in hand can use biodegradable pickup bags. They're all intended to keep your hands—and the environment—as clean as possible.

Biodegradable pickup bags are a green way to keep your block clean.

This pooper-scooper user leaves no dog doo behind.

GARBAGE TRUCKS

Ever heard of an inventor named George Dempster? If the answer is no, just swap out the first *e* in his last name with a *u*. You'll figure out why he's famous! In 1937 Dempster created the Dempster-Dumpster system. This setup allowed wheeled containers (or Dumpsters) to be mechanically tipped into waste-removal trucks. Dempster's invention was a major step in garbage removal. People had been trying to figure out new and more efficient ways to toss trash for ages.

Starting in the fourteenth century, "rakers," or early garbagemen, raked up garbage from the streets of medieval Europe. As time passed, people (and sometimes horses) hauled rubbish to the nearest landfill or dumping ground with the help of pull carts. During the 1900s, people began using motorized trucks to carry trash from neighborhoods to nearby dumps.

These days, most garbage trucks feature massive hydraulic (liquid-powered) arms and blades. Drivers can operate these parts from inside the vehicle. The parts lift and pack trash. Just how powerful are modern trucks? Well, some models are capable of raising and dumping 300-gallon (1,135-liter) containers!

If you're trying to wrap your head around that figure, check out a 10-gallon (38-liter) fish tank at the pet store. Then imagine filling that tank—and twenty-nine others like it—with junk. Yup, you'd be looking at more than a ton of trash. Which is exactly what certain garbage trucks are designed to hoist!

PARIS, FRANCE, USED TO BE A PARADISE FOR CARELESS DOG OWNERS. Instead of holding people responsible for their pets' messes, the city used a fleet of specially designed motorcycles to keep the streets free of animal waste. Each neon-green motorbike came with a suction machine (like a mini vacuum) for collection and cleanup. But these snazzy scooters took care of only about 20 percent of the city's dog feces. In 2002 Paris took up a more effective plan: handing out hefty fines to owners who refuse to scoop.

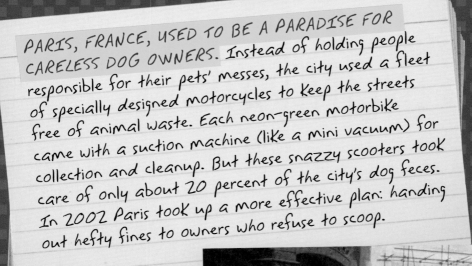

London "dustmen" take care of waste in the 1950s.

This modern garbage truck uses hydraulic arms to lift a Dumpster.

INCINERATORS

Picture this: you wake up in bed. It's a sunny morning. You stretch your arms, lean out the window . . . and see heaps of stinky garbage sitting in the street. Sound like a nightmare? Well, hundreds of years ago, that's exactly what you might have seen beyond your window.

In Europe and elsewhere, people didn't always have trustworthy ways to get rid of waste. Garbage often just sat around. These mountains of trash did more than cause people to pinch their noses. They also became breeding grounds for rats. And these pests sometimes spread fatal diseases. Fortunately, Albert Fryer of Nottingham, England, had a breakthrough. In the 1870s, Fryer developed the Destructor. Fryer's invention wasn't a killer robot or a folktale beast. It was an incinerator.

Incinerators are furnaces designed to burn waste. Early incinerators were often lined with brick and held metal grates inside. Waste burned between the brick walls until it turned to ash and gas. More than a century later, these devices are still in use.

Modern incinerators are more high tech, with moving parts and safety measures. But they still do the job of burning up stinky stuff. Early incinerator models can harm the environment if they burn the wrong thing by letting nasty chemicals into the air. So newer incinerators have ways to keep these chemicals contained. Some even help generate power.

Hospitals rely on incinerators to sterilize and eliminate roughly 90 percent of all medical waste, including bloody bandages, surgical gloves, and even body parts! (You may be grossed out, but would you really want that stuff laying in a landfill near your house? We didn't think so.)

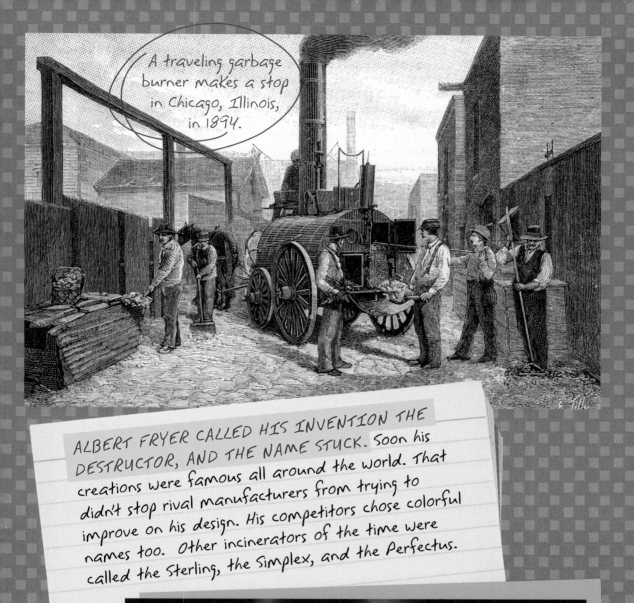

A traveling garbage burner makes a stop in Chicago, Illinois, in 1894.

ALBERT FRYER CALLED HIS INVENTION THE DESTRUCTOR, AND THE NAME STUCK. Soon his creations were famous all around the world. That didn't stop rival manufacturers from trying to improve on his design. His competitors chose colorful names too. Other incinerators of the time were called the Sterling, the Simplex, and the Perfectus.

This modern incineration plant uses extreme heat to destroy waste.

LANDFILLS

The ancient Greeks saw part of the bigger picture when it came to waste disposal. Okay, so recycling wasn't all the rage in 3000 B.C.E. Yet people in the Greek island of Crete devised a clever way to get rid of trash. Many experts believe the people of Crete dug large holes for waste. Next, they filled the holes with alternating levels of garbage and dirt. Some say the Cretans developed the world's earliest landfills.

Not everything can be recycled. Materials such as used tissues or diapers are too dirty or germ-covered to be reused. Materials such as Styrofoam can't be broken down by most recycling facilities. This is where landfills come in.

What's the big difference between a landfill and a plain old dump? Garbage in a landfill is crushed and then covered with layers of dirt. This way, rubbish is contained and controlled. It's also less likely to be a hot spot for bugs, rodents, and bacteria.

At a certain point, every landfill gets, well, filled. People have put everything from ski slopes to golf courses on top of these used-up landfills. But there is a downside to this type of waste management. Not all the items in a landfill are biodegradable. Other items break down in a manner that

harms the environment. And the lack of oxygen and microorganisms in a landfill often make it difficult for trash to break down naturally. Want slightly stinky proof of this fact? Talk to the researchers who toured a landfill and discovered twenty-five-year-old hot dogs, corncobs, and grapes!

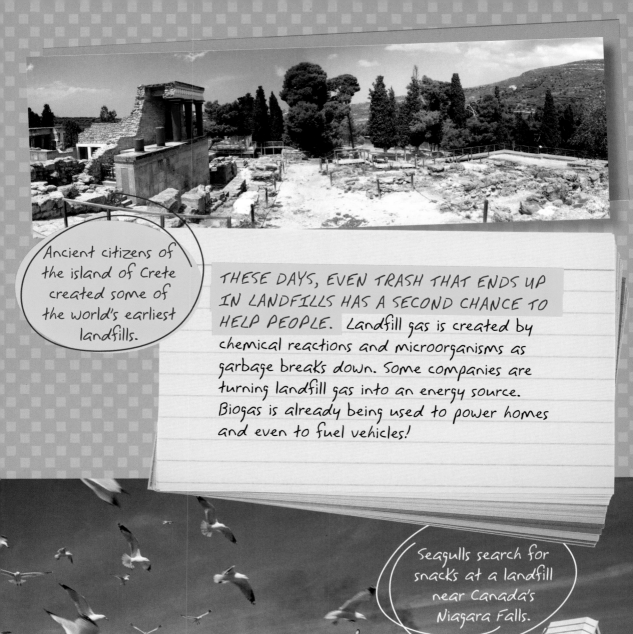

Ancient citizens of the island of Crete created some of the world's earliest landfills.

THESE DAYS, EVEN TRASH THAT ENDS UP IN LANDFILLS HAS A SECOND CHANCE TO HELP PEOPLE. Landfill gas is created by chemical reactions and microorganisms as garbage breaks down. Some companies are turning landfill gas into an energy source. Biogas is already being used to power homes and even to fuel vehicles!

Seagulls search for snacks at a landfill near Canada's Niagara Falls.

GARBAGE DISPOSALS

John W. Hammes of Racine, Wisconsin, wore many hats. He was an architect, an inventor, and a man who wasn't afraid to get his hands (and feet) dirty! Hammes designed the earliest model of the modern garbage disposal. He was hoping to find a better way to get rid of food waste. Starting in 1927, he dedicated eleven years to perfecting the InSinkErator. He often had to wade through pools of liquid waste along the way. How else could Hammes examine the size of food particles that had been chopped up by his invention and forced through his kitchen plumbing?

In the end, this rather sloppy science paid off. Hammes patented his disposal in 1935. He established a company to build and sell it a few years later. Even then, garbage disposals weren't an instant hit. Some critics predicted that plunking food waste into the plumbing would create problems within community sewer systems. Certain cities banned garbage disposals until later in the twentieth century.

These days, garbage disposals are found in roughly half of all U.S. homes. Many Americans view them as an easy way to prevent old food from stinking up trash cans and creating pest problems. So what's the catch? Users need a steady grip. From rocks to wedding rings, plenty of items have been dropped or gotten stuck in Hammes's invention. In 2002 an adventurous cat named Rudy got his whole head caught inside a garbage disposal. It took a visit from the fire department, the removal of the entire sink, and a trip to the vet (sink and all) to get Rudy free.

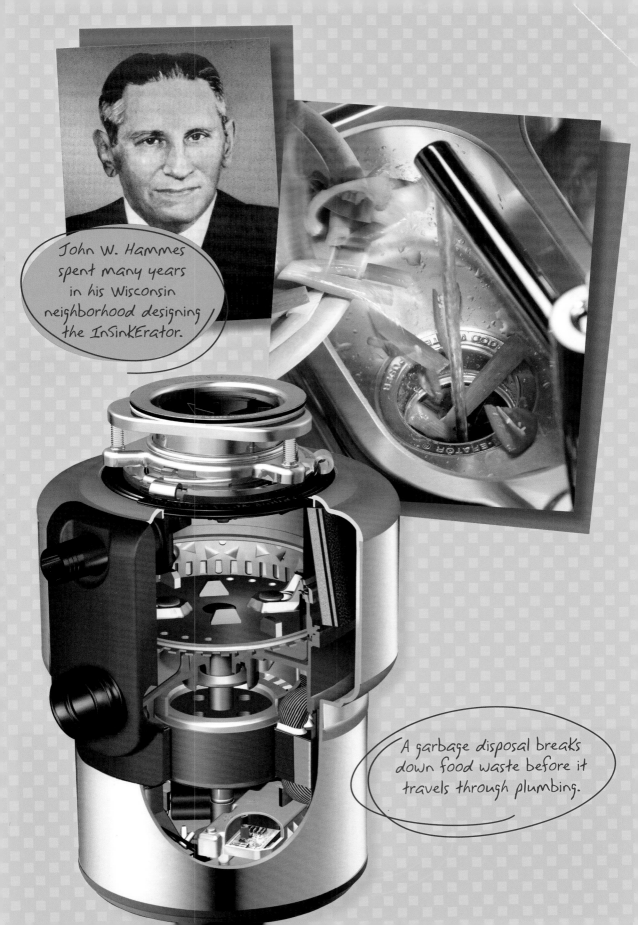

John W. Hammes spent many years in his Wisconsin neighborhood designing the InSinkErator.

A garbage disposal breaks down food waste before it travels through plumbing.

AIR FRESHENERS

Pine forests, lavender fields, citrus fruits . . . the list of scents that you can shoot from a can goes on and on. Modern people have the power to make their cars or living rooms smell like tropical beaches or orange groves. The public was introduced to air fresheners as we know them in the late 1940s. But people have been trying to figure out how to eliminate not-so-awesome odors for far longer.

Thousands of years ago, ancient Egyptians used flowers, herbs, and spices to keep their tombs smelling spiffy. Thousands of years later, inventors figured out that flowery-smelling mists could be released into the air. They used the same technology that the U.S. military had relied on to spray bug-killing pesticides.

Inventors didn't stop there! Americans first began buying aerosol air fresheners in 1948. Since then, manufacturers have come up with ways to cut costs, improve odor control, and go green. Still, some critics note that common air fresheners can pollute the environment and harm human health. So how do these experts advise that you get rid of the stench of sweaty socks or the moldy cheese sandwich that you found under your bed? Well, some of the oldest natural air fresheners are still the best.

One natural solution is potpourri, a blend of dried flowers, herbs, and oils. Another is pomanders. People make pomanders by poking holes in an orange or an apple, stuffing cloves into the holes, rolling the fruit in some cinnamon or nutmeg, and baking it in the oven. People once carried around these fruity perfume balls to mask their body odors. These days, you can leave them in a bowl or hang them from the ceiling to keep your home smelling fresh.

Aerosol air fresheners helped hide stinky food smells in the mid-twentieth century.

Potpourri is a natural way to block odors.

GLOSSARY

aerosol: a substance that is kept under pressure and released as a spray

alternating: moving between one thing and another

bacteria: microscopic life-forms, some of which cause diseases in humans and animals

biodegrade: to break down naturally

cesspool: an underground storage area for liquid waste

disinfect: to free from germs by cleaning

fecal: related to human or animal waste

hydraulic: running on or operated by waterpower

incinerator: a furnace or container that burns waste materials to ash

landfill: a place where waste is buried between layers of earth

microorganism: a very tiny living thing, such as a bacterium

patent: the exclusive right to make, use, or sell an invention

pesticide: a toxic substance used to kill animal pests or harmful plants

septic: used for sewage treatment or disposal

sewage: solid or liquid waste material found in water

sterilize: to use chemicals to remove harmful microorganisms

valve: a tool that controls the movement of liquid through a pipe

FURTHER INFORMATION

Albee, Sarah. *Poop Happened!: A History of the World from the Bottom Up.* New York: Walker, 2010. Check out this book to learn more about how peoples throughout history have dealt with waste.

Facts about Garbage—Dialogue for Kids
http://idahoptv.org/dialogue4kids/season6/garbage/facts.cfm
Visit this site for information about how much garbage people make, where it goes, and ways to recycle.

Gregory, Morna E., and Sian James. *Toilets of the World.* New York: Merrell, 2009. Pick up this book to discover crazy names and designs for toilets from Japan, the Caribbean, New Zealand, and elsewhere.

Huey, Lois Minor. *Ick! Yuck! Eew! Our Gross American History.* Minneapolis: Millbrook Press, 2014. This fun book shows readers how yucky the past could be, highlighting nasty smells, sounds, and pests from early American life.

Sewer History (and Other Stinky Things)—Pima County Regional Wastewater Reclamation Department
http://www.pima.gov/wwm/Kids/history.htm
Take a journey through the history of outhouses or find out some strange facts about sewer history at this site.

Toilet History Timeline—Inventors Trunk
http://www.inventors-trunk.com/toilet-history-timeline.html
Visitors to this Inventors Trunk site can follow the history of the toilet from 1391 to the present, as well as learn some toilet fun facts.

Wastes—U.S. Environmental Protection Agency
http://www.epa.gov/osw/education/kids/index.htm
This site from the Environmental Protection Agency has waste-related suggestions about how to protect the planet.

Zamosky, Lisa. *Sanitation Workers Then and Now.* Huntington Beach, CA: Teacher Created Materials, 2008. Check out this book for facts and photos about the jobs of sanitation workers and how they have changed over time.

INDEX

PHOTO ACKNOWLEDGMENTS

The images in this book are used with the permission of:
© iStockphoto.com/Huguette Roe, p. 5 (top);
© iStockphoto.com/Geo Martinez, p. 5 (bottom);
© SCA Svenska Cellulosa Aktiebolaget, p. 7 (left);
© iStockphoto.com/Glenda Powers, p. 7 (right);
© ryanroderickbeiler.com, p. 9 (top); © iStockphoto.com/GaryAlvis, p. 9 (bottom); Mary Evans Picture Library/ Edwin Wallace/Everett Collection, p. 11 (main); © iStockphoto.com/Picsfive, p. 11 (inset); Marion O'Brien Donovan Papers, SI Photo 2000.5055, Archives Center, National Museum of American History, Smithsonian Institution, p. 13 (top); © iStockphoto.com/pekkak, p. 13 (center); © iStockphoto.com/arsenik, p. 13 (bottom); AP Photo/Steven Senne, p. 15 (top); © Pantheon/SuperStock, p. 15 (bottom); © Steve Lyne/Dorling Kindersley/Getty Images, p. 17 (top); AP Photo/The Salisbury Daily Times/Todd Dudek, p. 17 (bottom left); © BCritchley/Dreamstime.com, p. 17 (bottom right); © John Chillingworth/CORBIS, p. 19 (top); © Anthony Baggett/Dreamstime.com, p. 19 (bottom); Mary Evans Picture Library/Everett Collection, p. 21 (top); © iStockphoto.com/Michael Utech, p. 21 (bottom); © iStockphoto.com/Susana Guzmán Martínez, p. 23 (top); © Thomas Kitchin & Victoria Hurst/All Canada Photos/Getty Images, p. 23 (bottom); Courtesy of InSinkErator® business unit of Emerson Electric Co., p. 25 (all); © iStockphoto.com/Gennadiy Poznyakov, p. 27 (main); © Todd Strand/Independent Picture Service, p. 27 (inset); © SuperStock, p. 29 (top); © iStockphoto.com/stockcam, p. 29 (bottom left); © Studio544/Dreamstime.com, p. 29 (bottom right).
Front cover: © iStockphoto.com/Jennifer Sheets.

Main body text set in Highlander ITC Std Book 13/16.
Typeface provided by International Typeface Corp.

LERNER e SOURCE

Expand learning beyond the printed book. Download free, complementary educational resources for this book from our website, www.lernerresource.com.